# Oprah, In Her Words:
## Our American Princess

*"Tuchy" Palmieri*

ISBN: 1-4392-1862-5
ISBN-13: 9781439218624

Visit www.booksurge.com to order additional copies.

*To Oprah Winfrey, for being such an example of achievement on so many levels; for her contributions to mankind on so many levels; and for her commitment to personal growth for both herself and her followers; and lastly for being Our American Princess–a shining example of the American Dream being fulfilled.*

*To the people who support me in bringing the words of wisdom from all over the world, from the beginning of recorded time, and from the biggest pool of wisdom–the unknowns; the ordinary people.*

*To my best friend and wife, Susie; our children, Kathleen, Philip, Amy, John, and Stephan; our grandchildren, Sean, Alicia, Heather, Julia, Olivia, C.J., Jack, Will, Julia (Tiny II), Ava, Chris, Sophia, and Adeline.*

*To our parents, Josephine and Jean, and our brother and sisters Chips, Liz, Lucia, Mary, and Flo. Last but not least, to each and every buyer of my books that help keep my dream alive.*

*May the words of Oprah–the suggested affirmations, inquiries, and actions–make a contribution to the people who read them.*

*Please note that while the quotes are from Oprah Winfrey and acknowledged as such, the contents of the book are from Tuchy and are not endorsed by Oprah Winfrey.*

## HEALTH AND WELL-BEING

*Oprah Winfrey–"Before you agree to do anything that might add even the smallest amount of stress to your life, ask yourself: What is my truest intention? Give yourself time to let a 'yes' resound within you. When it's right, I guarantee that your entire body will feel it."*

Suggested Affirmation: "I reduce stress in my life by checking in with my body."

Suggested Inquiry: How does your body feel?

Suggested Action: Relieve stress with quiet time each morning.

*Oprah Winfrey—"As you become more clear about who you really are, you'll be better able to decide what is best for you–the first time around."*

Suggested Affirmation: "I trust myself; my first decisions are the best."

Suggested Inquiry: Is there anything you need to get clear on?

Suggested Action: Pray for clarity when needed.

## HEALTH AND WELL-BEING

My affirmations:

_____

_____

_____

_____

What I am inquiring into:

_____

_____

_____

_____

My planned actions:

_____

_____

_____

_____

## HEALTH AND WELL-BEING

*Oprah Winfrey– "Breathe. Let go. And remind yourself that this very moment is the only one you know you have for sure."*

Suggested Affirmation: "I let go by stepping back and breathing."

Suggested Inquiry: Are you living in the moment?

Suggested Action: Forgive yourself for past mistakes and let it go.

*Oprah Winfrey– "I finally realized that being grateful to my body was key to giving more love to myself."*

Suggested Affirmation: "I am grateful for my body as it works for me."

Suggested Inquiry: Are you truly grateful for your body?

Suggested Action: Treat your body to a hot bath, massage, or facial.

## HEALTH AND WELL-BEING

My affirmations:

_____

_____

_____

_____

What I am inquiring into:

_____

_____

_____

_____

My planned actions:

_____

_____

_____

_____

## HEALTH AND WELL-BEING

*Oprah Winfrey– "If you neglect to recharge a battery, it dies. And if you run full speed ahead without stopping for water, you lose momentum to finish the race."*

Suggested Affirmation: "I recharge my body whenever it is needed."

Suggested Inquiry: What can you do for yourself to recharge your batteries?

Suggested Action: Recharge your batteries with rest.

*Oprah Winfrey– "You can take from every experience what it has to offer you. And you cannot be defeated if you just keep taking one breath followed by another."*

Suggested Affirmation: "I cannot be defeated."

Suggested Inquiry: What are you taking from this experience?

Suggested Action: Keep breathing.

## ADVICE AND ENCOURAGEMENT

My affirmations:

_____

_____

_____

_____

What I am inquiring into:

_____

_____

_____

_____

My planned actions:

_____

_____

_____

_____

## ADVICE AND ENCOURAGEMENT

*Oprah Winfrey– "My philosophy is that not only are you responsible for your life, but doing the best at this moment puts you in the best place for the next moment."*

Suggested Affirmation: "I am responsible for my life, and I do my best at this moment."

Suggested Inquiry: Where in my life am I not being responsible?

Suggested Action: Take responsibility for an aspect of your life that you are not being responsible for.

*Oprah Winfrey– "Real integrity is doing the right thing, knowing that nobody's going to know whether you did it or not."*

Suggested Affirmation: "I maintain my integrity by doing the right thing regardless as to others' knowledge of my actions."

Suggested Inquiry: Inquire into the question that God knows everything you do.

Suggested Action: Do something good for someone without anyone knowing about it.

## ADVICE AND ENCOURAGEMENT

My affirmations:

_____

_____

_____

_____

What I am inquiring into:

_____

_____

_____

_____

My planned actions:

_____

_____

_____

_____

## ADVICE AND ENCOURAGEMENT

*Oprah Winfrey– "You can have it all. You just can't have it all at once."*

Suggested Affirmation: "I can have it all in due time."

Suggested Inquiry: Inquire into the possibility that your words can help or hinder what you can have.

Suggested Action: Develop an action plan for what you want.

*Oprah Winfrey– "I do not know what the future holds but I know who holds the future."*

Suggested Affirmation: "I hold the future in my hands."

Suggested Inquiry: Inquire into the possibility that your future is impacted by the way you speak about it.

Suggested Action: Do or say something today that brings a good future.

## ADVICE AND ENCOURAGEMENT

My affirmations:

_____

_____

_____

_____

What I am inquiring into:

_____

_____

_____

_____

My planned actions:

_____

_____

_____

_____

## ADVICE AND ENCOURAGMENT

*Oprah Winfrey– "Be more splendid; more extraordinary. Use every moment to fill yourself up."*

Suggested Affirmation: "I am more splendid and extraordinary than I was yesterday."

Suggested Inquiry: Into the possibility that action makes you extraordinary.

Suggested Action: Do something that is extraordinary for you.

*Oprah Winfrey– "Become the change you want to see–those are words I live by."*

Suggested Affirmation: "I am becoming the positive change I want to be."

Suggested Inquiry: Into the thought that deciding to change is in itself an action.

Suggested Action: Make at least one change today towards becoming who you want to be.

## ADVICE AND ENCOURAGEMENT

My affirmations:

_____

_____

_____

_____

What I am inquiring into:

_____

_____

_____

_____

My planned actions:

_____

_____

_____

_____

## ADVICE AND ENCOURAGEMENT

*Oprah Winfrey– "Every time you state what you want or believe, you're the first to hear it. It's a message to both you and others about what you think is possible. Don't put a ceiling on yourself."*

Suggested Affirmation: "I say what I want and do not put a ceiling on myself."

Suggested Inquiry: Into the thought that your words can empower you or disempower you. Ask yourself, "What words empower me?"

Suggested Action: Today say what is right for you and true for you after considering its effect on others.

*Oprah Winfrey– "Partake of some of life's sweet pleasures. And yes, get comfortable with yourself."*

Suggested Affirmation: "I partake of some of life's sweet pleasures. I am comfortable with myself."

Suggested Inquiry: What can I do to be more comfortable with myself?

Suggested Action: Do something that makes you more comfortable with yourself.

## ADVICE AND ENCOURAGEMENT

My affirmations:

_____

_____

_____

_____

What I am inquiring into:

_____

_____

_____

_____

My planned actions:

_____

_____

_____

_____

## ADVICE AND ENCOURAGEMENT

*Oprah Winfrey– "The biggest adventure you can ever take is to live the life of your dreams."*

Suggested Affirmation: "I live the life of my dreams."

Suggested Inquiry: Into what your dreams are today.

Suggested Action: Do one thing that takes you one step closer to one of your dreams.

*Oprah Winfrey– "You are built not to shrink down to less but to blossom into more."*

Suggested Affirmation: "I blossom and bloom more each day."

Suggested Inquiry: Into the possibility that action causes blooming and blossoming.

Suggested Action: Do whatever you were doing, just do it a little better than the last time you did it.

*Oprah Winfrey– "You are what you are by what you believe!"*

Suggested Affirmation: "I believe the sky is the limit."

Suggested Inquiry: Who puts the limits on you?

Suggested Action: Do something you were not sure you could do.

## ADVICE AND ENCOURAGEMENT

My affirmations:

_____

_____

_____

_____

What I am inquiring into:

_____

_____

_____

_____

My planned actions:

_____

_____

_____

_____

## ADVICE AND ENCOURAGEMENT

*Oprah Winfrey– "We are each responsible for our own life–no other person is or even can be."*

Suggested Affirmation: "I am responsible for my own life."

Suggested Inquiry: If I'm not responsible for my own life then who is?

Suggested Action: Take responsibility in your life where you were not being responsible.

*Oprah Winfrey– "We can't become what we need to be by remaining what we are."*

Suggested Affirmation: "I am becoming who I need to be by letting go of who I have been."

Suggested Inquiry: Into the thought that letting go and letting God helps one become who they need to be.

Suggested Action: Stop and/or start something that is moving you towards becoming who you need to be.

*Oprah Winfrey– "Don't live your life to please other people."*

Suggested Affirmation: "I live my life to please myself not others."

Suggested Inquiry: Into the thought that helping others pleases and that pleasing others hurts.

Suggested Action: Do something that puts you first today.

## ADVICE AND ENCOURAGEMENT

My affirmations:

_____

_____

_____

_____

What I am inquiring into:

_____

_____

_____

_____

My planned actions:

_____

_____

_____

_____

## ADVICE AND ENCOURAGEMENT

*Oprah Winfrey– "Devote today to something so daring even you can't believe you're doing it."*

Suggested Affirmation: "I do things so daring that at first I do not believe it's me doing them."

Suggested Inquiry: What would life look like for you being a daredevil?

Suggested Action: Do something today that you do not believe you would do.

*Oprah Winfrey– "When someone shows you who they are, believe them the first time."*

Suggested Affirmation: "I believe people are who they show me they are."

Suggested Inquiry: Into the thought that people will show you who they are if they trust you.

Suggested Action: Show people who you really are.

## ADVICE AND ENCOURAGEMENT

My affirmations:

_____

_____

_____

_____

What I am inquiring into:

_____

_____

_____

_____

My planned actions:

_____

_____

_____

_____

## ADVICE AND ENCOURAGEMENT

*Oprah Winfrey– "Your true passion should feel like breathing; it's that natural."*

Suggested Affirmation: "My true passion feels like breathing to me."

Suggested Inquiry: Is what I am currently doing feeling easy to me?

Suggested Action: Spend some time today doing what is my true passion.

*Oprah Winfrey– "Always continue the climb. It is possible for you to do whatever you choose, if you first get to know who you are and are willing to work with a power that is greater than ourselves to do it."*

Suggested Affirmation: "I am always climbing."

Suggested Inquiry: Into the possibility that the only limits are based on my thinking.

Suggested Action: Climb closer to God today.

## ADVICE AND ENCOURAGEMENT

My affirmations:

_____

_____

_____

_____

What I am inquiring into:

_____

_____

_____

_____

My planned actions:

_____

_____

_____

_____

## ADVICE AND ENCOURAGEMENT

*Oprah Winfrey– "Never take a 'no' from somebody who isn't in a position to give you a 'yes' in the first place."*

Suggested Affirmation: "I never take 'no' from somebody who isn't in a position to say 'yes' in the first place."

Suggested Inquiry: Into the question, "How much more peaceful would life be if you only communicated with those who can do something?"

Suggested Action: Be courteous, and not engage anyone who is only a messenger or a bystander.

*Oprah Winfrey– "If you believe you can only go so far, it is an obstacle."*

Suggested Affirmation: "All things are possible because I believe."

Suggested Inquiry: Into the possibility that you can do more and go farther than you think you can.

Suggested Action: Take action and trust in God.

## ADVICE AND ENCOURAGEMENT

My affirmations:

_____

_____

_____

_____

What I am inquiring into:

_____

_____

_____

_____

My planned actions:

_____

_____

_____

_____

## ADVICE AND ENCOURAGMENT

*Oprah Winfrey– "Pay attention to your feelings. The path to discovering why you are here is through your feelings."*

Suggested Affirmation: "I pay attention to my feelings."

Suggested Inquiry: Into the thought that you are not your feelings and that your feelings are neither good nor bad.

Suggested Action: Feel your feelings and not cover them or numb them with addictions, food, alcohol, drugs, etc.

*Oprah Winfrey– "I don't believe in coincidences."*

Suggested Affirmation: "I do not believe in coincidences."

Suggested Inquiry: Into the thought that what happens, happens.

Suggested Action: Write down what happens today that looks like a coincidence, and is not.

*Oprah Winfrey– "Forgiveness is letting go of the hope that the past can be changed."*

Suggested Affirmation: "I forgive and let go of wanting to change the past."

Suggested Inquiry: Is it possible to change the past?

Suggested Action: Forgive someone for past actions or inactions.

## ADVICE AND ENCOURAGEMENT

My affirmations:

_____

_____

_____

_____

What I am inquiring into:

_____

_____

_____

_____

My planned actions:

_____

_____

_____

_____

## ADVICE AND ENCOURAGEMENT

*Oprah Winfrey– "You cannot hate other people without hating yourself."*

Suggested Affirmation: "I love others as I love myself."

Suggested Inquiry: Look into the possibility that resentment is a form of attachment.

Suggested Action: Write a forgiveness letter. Review it with someone close to you. Forgive that person and pray for them.

*Oprah Winfrey– "Follow your instincts. That's where true wisdom manifests itself."*

Suggested Affirmation: "I follow my true instincts."

Suggested Inquiry: Into the possibility that my instincts are the wisest.

Suggested Action: Listen to and follow your instinct at least one more time today than you did yesterday.

## SUCCESS

My affirmations:

_____

_____

_____

_____

What I am inquiring into:

_____

_____

_____

_____

My planned actions:

_____

_____

_____

_____

## SUCCESS

*Oprah Winfrey– "There's no such thing as failure. Mistakes happen in your life to bring into focus more clearly who you really are."*

Suggested Affirmation: "I do not believe in failure."

Suggested Inquiry: Do I always get a result whenever I attempt something?

Suggested Action: Pick an area or activity in your life in which you got a result that was not what you wanted; change what you do and get another result.

*Oprah Winfrey– "Think like a queen. A queen is not afraid to fail. Failure is another stepping stone to greatness."*

Suggested Affirmation: "I think like a Queen/King, and I am not afraid to fail. I use my failures as stepping stones."

Suggested Inquiry: Into the thought that the more you fail, the more you succeed.

Suggested Action: When you make mistakes this week, write them down and discover what you learned from them.

## SUCCESS

My affirmations:

_____

_____

_____

_____

What I am inquiring into:

_____

_____

_____

_____

My planned actions:

_____

_____

_____

_____

## SUCCESS

*Oprah Winfrey– "Challenges are gifts that force us to search for a new center of gravity. Don't fight them. Just find a different way to stand."*

Suggested Affirmation: "I accept challenges as a way to grow."

Suggested Inquiry: Look into the possibility that challenges make life worthwhile.

Suggested Action: Take something that challenges you and write what growth will occur as you meet the challenge.

*Oprah Winfrey—"Cheers to a new year and another chance for us to get it right."*

Suggested Affirmation: "I look at a new year knowing that progress will be made in all areas of my life."

Suggested Inquiry: Am I complete with last year?

Suggested Action: Write down all your accomplishments. Complete with any area in which you did not finish or accomplish.

## SUCCESS

My affirmations:

_____

_____

_____

_____

What I am inquiring into:

_____

_____

_____

_____

My planned actions:

_____

_____

_____

_____

## SUCCESS

*Oprah Winfrey—"Do the one thing you think you cannot do. Fail at it. Try again. Do better the second time. The only people who never tumble are those who never mount the high wire. This is your moment. Own it."*

Suggested Affirmation: "I will do something today that I think I may not be able to do."

Suggested Inquiry: Into the possibility that when you say you can't or when you say you can, you are right.

Suggested Action: Do one thing that you thought you could not do.

*Oprah Winfrey—"Doing the best at this moment puts you in the best place for the next moment."*

Suggested Affirmation: "I do my best this very moment."

Suggested Inquiry: What do I need to do better?

Suggested Action: Take something you did not do your best at and improve on it.

## SUCCESS

My affirmations:

_____

_____

_____

_____

What I am inquiring into:

_____

_____

_____

_____

My planned actions:

_____

_____

_____

_____

## SUCCESS

*Oprah Winfrey– "Energy is the essence of life. Every day you decide how you're going to use it by knowing what you want and what it takes to reach that goal, and by maintaining focus."*

Suggested Affirmation: "I use my energy efficiently to allow me to reach my goals."

Suggested Inquiry: Where do you want to expend your energy in order to maximize the achievement of your goals?

Suggested Action: Eliminate one energy drain in your life. Do one thing that energizes you.

*Oprah Winfrey– "I do not believe in failure. It is not failure if you enjoyed the process."*

Suggested Affirmation: "The only failure is when I stop trying."

Suggested Inquiry: Do you believe that you only fail when you stop trying?

Suggested Action: Restart some goal or activity you gave up on.

## SUCCESS

My affirmations:

_____

_____

_____

_____

What I am inquiring into:

_____

_____

_____

_____

My planned actions:

_____

_____

_____

_____

## SUCCESS

*Oprah Winfrey– "The big secret in life is that there is no big secret. Whatever your goal, you can get there if you're willing to work."*

Suggested Affirmation: "I know that there are no big secrets in life."

Suggested Inquiry: What are your secrets in life?

Suggested Action: Take a project or goal in which you have had no movement because you do not know the secret. Take some action on it.

*Oprah Winfrey– "The key to realizing a dream is to focus not on success but on significance, and then even the small steps and little victories along your path will take on greater meaning."*

Suggested Affirmation: "I realize my dreams by taking small steps and by making them significant."

Suggested Inquiry: What small steps and little victories can I take?

Suggested Action: Write down the small steps and little victories you will have towards the pursuit of your goal.

*Oprah Winfrey– "With every experience, you alone are painting your own canvas; thought by thought, choice by choice."*

Suggested Affirmation: "I am the painter of my life."

Suggested Inquiry: What can I do to paint differently?

Suggested Action: Have bright thoughts and make light choices.

## SUCCESS

My affirmations:

_____

_____

_____

_____

What I am inquiring into:

_____

_____

_____

_____

My planned actions:

_____

_____

_____

_____

## SUCCESS

*Oprah Winfrey– "Failure is defined by our reaction to it."*

Suggested Affirmation: "I react to failure in a positive way, knowing that my next attempt may be successful because of it."

Suggested Inquiry: How can you react to failure in such a way that the failure is not felt?

Suggested Action: Fail in a new way.

*Oprah Winfrey– "Luck is a matter of preparation meeting opportunity."*

Suggested Affirmation: "I am lucky because I am prepared when opportunity knocks."

Suggested Inquiry: What do I need to do to be prepared?

Suggested Action: Prepare for the lucky break by being in action today.

*Oprah Winfrey– "Triumph is just 'umph' added to 'try.'"*

Suggested Affirmation: "I put 'umph' in everything I try so that more often than not I triumph."

Suggested Inquiry: What are ways 'umph' expresses itself?

Suggested Action: Try to pick up a pencil.

**SUCCESS**

My affirmations:

_____

_____

_____

_____

What I am inquiring into:

_____

_____

_____

_____

My planned actions:

_____

_____

_____

_____

## SUCCESS

*Oprah Winfrey– "You know you are on the road to success if you would do your job and not be paid for it."*

Suggested Affirmation: "I do what I love and know success will follow."

Suggested Inquiry: Am I doing what I love?

Suggested Action: Spend some time doing what you love to do.

*Oprah Winfrey– "Think like a queen. A queen is not afraid to fail. Failure is another stepping stone to greatness."*

Suggested Affirmation: "There is no such thing as failure."

Suggested Inquiry: Do you always get a result when you try something?

Suggested Action: Fail in a new way.

*Oprah Winfrey– "I've come to believe that each of us has a personal calling that's as unique as a fingerprint, and that the best way to succeed is to discover what you love and then find a way to offer it to others in the form of service, working hard, and also allowing the energy of the universe to lead you."*

Suggested Affirmation: "I am discovering what I love and what my personal calling is."

Suggested Inquiry: What can I offer?

Suggested Action: Discover something new today that you love.

## FRIENDSHIP LOVE

My affirmations:

_____

_____

_____

_____

What I am inquiring into:

_____

_____

_____

_____

My planned actions:

_____

_____

_____

_____

## FRIENDSHIP LOVE

*Oprah Winfrey– "Lots of people want to ride with you in the limo, but what you want is someone who will take the bus with you when the limo breaks down."*

Suggested Affirmation: "I take the bus with others when their limo breaks down."

Suggested Inquiry: Who in your life will take the bus with you when the limo breaks down?

Suggested Action: Find someone whose limo broke down and take the bus with them.

*Oprah Winfrey– "Surround yourself only with people who are going to lift you higher."*

Suggested Affirmation: "I surround myself with people better than I and who will lift me up."

Suggested Inquiry: Who lifts you higher? Who pulls you down?

Suggested Action: Make a new friend of someone who lifts you higher.

## FRIENDSHIP LOVE

My affirmations:

_____

_____

_____

_____

What I am inquiring into:

_____

_____

_____

_____

My planned actions:

_____

_____

_____

_____

**FRIENDSHIP LOVE**

*Oprah Winfrey– "Every one of us gets through the tough times because somebody is there, standing in the gap to close it for us."*

Suggested Affirmation: "I have friends and God to help me through tough times."

Suggested Inquiry: Who stands in the gap to close it for you?

Suggested Action: Go stand in the gap for someone who is having a tough time.

*Oprah Winfrey– "For every one of us that succeeds, it's because there's somebody there to show you the way out. The light doesn't always necessarily have to be in your family; for me it was teachers and school."*

Suggested Affirmation: "My light comes from many different people."

Suggested Inquiry: Who are the people who shine lights on you?

Suggested Action: Thank the person(s) who shine the light on you.

**FRIENDSHIP LOVE**

My affirmations:

_____

_____

_____

_____

What I am inquiring into:

_____

_____

_____

_____

My planned actions:

_____

_____

_____

_____

## FRIENDSHIP LOVE

*Oprah Winfrey– "My idea of heaven is a great big baked potato and someone to share it with."*

Suggested Affirmation: "Heaven is sharing with people."

Suggested Inquiry: Who are those special someones to share the simple moments in life with?

Suggested Action: Go share some special pleasures with someone.

*Oprah Winfrey– "Let your light shine. Shine within you so that it can shine on someone else. Let your light shine."*

Suggested Affirmation: "My light shines within me."

Suggested Inquiry: What ways can you show your light so that it shines on people?

Suggested Action: Smile, keep you head up, and help others.

## FRIENDSHIP LOVE

My affirmations:

_____

_____

_____

_____

What I am inquiring into:

_____

_____

_____

_____

My planned actions:

_____

_____

_____

_____

**FRIENDSHIP LOVE**

*Oprah Winfrey– "The roses, the lovely notes, the dining and dancing are all welcome and splendid. But when the Godiva is gone, the gift of real love is having someone who'll go the distance with you. Someone who, when the wedding day limo breaks down, is willing to share a seat on the bus."*

Suggested Affirmation: "I go the distance with my love."

Suggested Inquiry: How far are you willing to go when the limo breaks down?

Suggested Action: Give the gift of real love by being there for your loved one(s).

*Oprah Winfrey– "Mr. Right is coming. But he's in Africa and he's walking."*

Suggested Affirmation: "Miss/Mr. Right is coming."

Suggested Inquiry: What qualities does Mr./Ms. Right need to have?

Suggested Action: Write down the qualities that you want in Mr./Ms. Right.

## FRIENDSHIP LOVE

My affirmations:

_____

_____

_____

_____

What I am inquiring into:

_____

_____

_____

_____

My planned actions:

_____

_____

_____

_____

**FRIENDSHIP LOVE**

*Oprah Winfrey– "I don't think you ever stop giving. I really don't. I think it's an on-going process. And it's not just about being able to write a check. It's being able to touch somebody's life."*

Suggested Affirmation: "I touch someone's life each day."

Suggested Inquiry: What are your thoughts about giving?

Suggested Action: Touch someone today by giving.

*Oprah Winfrey– "I'm easy to look at, but so hard to see."*

Suggested Affirmation: "I am easy to look at and easy to see."

Suggested Inquiry: What must one do or how must one be to be easy to see?

Suggested Action: Let down your mask and be who you are.

## FRIENDSHIP LOVE

My affirmations:

_____

_____

_____

_____

What I am inquiring into:

_____

_____

_____

_____

My planned actions:

_____

_____

_____

_____

## FRIENDSHIP LOVE

*Oprah Winfrey– "When you give up on life, never give up on yourself, because there is so much for you to keep on giving."*

Suggested Affirmation: "I do not give up on myself and that makes life worthwhile."

Suggested Inquiry: Inquire into the thought that giving makes life worthwhile.

Suggested Action: Affirm that life is good; life is a gift from God.

*Oprah Winfrey– "Don't back down just to keep the peace. Standing up for your beliefs builds self-confidence and self-esteem."*

Suggested Affirmation: "I stand up for what I believe."

Suggested Inquiry: Does standing up for one's beliefs build self-confidence and self-esteem?

Suggested Action: Write down where in your life you are not standing up, then take some small action towards standing up regarding one of those issues.

## GROWTH

My affirmations:

_____

_____

_____

_____

What I am inquiring into:

_____

_____

_____

_____

My planned actions:

_____

_____

_____

_____

## GROWTH

*Oprah Winfrey– "Everything in your world is created by what you think."*

Suggested Affirmation: "My thoughts and words create my world."

Suggested Inquiry: What thoughts make my world good and what thoughts make my world bad?

Suggested Action: Write down words that empower you and words that make your world great.

*Oprah Winfrey– "I don't think of myself as a poor deprived ghetto girl who made good. I think of myself as somebody who from an early age knew I was responsible for myself, and I had to make good."*

Suggested Affirmation: "I take responsibility for myself, and I am making good."

Suggested Inquiry: Into the thought that suffering occurs when we are not being responsible.

Suggested Action: Take some responsibility in an area of your life in which you are suffering.

**GROWTH**

My affirmations:

_____

_____

_____

_____

What I am inquiring into:

_____

_____

_____

_____

My planned actions:

_____

_____

_____

_____

## GROWTH

*Oprah Winfrey– "All these years I've been feeling like I was growing into myself. Finally, I feel grown."*

Suggested Affirmation: "I am growing into myself."

Suggested Inquiry: Do I feel grown?

Suggested Action: Read, do a workshop, attend a seminar on personal growth.

*Oprah Winfrey– "Books were my pass to personal freedom. I learned to read at age three, and soon discovered there was a whole world to conquer that went beyond our farm in Mississippi."*

Suggested Affirmation: "I read and listen to educational programs as my pass to freedom."

Suggested Inquiry: How can reading and listening to educational programs bring me freedom?

Suggested Action: Do something freeing today.

## GROWTH

My affirmations:

_____

_____

_____

_____

What I am inquiring into:

_____

_____

_____

_____

My planned actions:

_____

_____

_____

_____

## GROWTH

*Oprah Winfrey– "If you want your life to be more rewarding, you have to change the way you think."*

Suggested Affirmation: "I am always upgrading my thinking to make life more rewarding."

Suggested Inquiry: Can life get rewarding for me by simply changing my thinking?

Suggested Action: Catch yourself when you have a thought that does not make life rewarding and cancel it by replacing it with speaking and thinking differently such that life becomes rewarding.

*Oprah Winfrey– "Every time you suppress some part of yourself or allow others to play you small, you are in essence ignoring the owner's manual your creator gave you and destroying your design."*

Suggested Affirmation: "I am the best me there is and I express myself fully; spiritually, emotionally, and physically."

Suggested Inquiry: How do I allow others to play me small?

Suggested Action: Ask God for help in being all He wants you to be.

## GROWTH

My affirmations:

_____

_____

_____

_____

What I am inquiring into:

_____

_____

_____

_____

My planned actions:

_____

_____

_____

_____

## GROWTH

*Oprah Winfrey– "Challenges are gifts that force us to search for a new center of gravity. Don't fight them. Just find a different way to stand."*

Suggested Affirmation: "I accept challenges as a way to grow."

Suggested Inquiry: How do I shift from fighting challenges to accepting challenges as a way to grow?

Suggested Action: Thank God for the challenges of the day, and ask Him to be with you.

*Oprah Winfrey– "Be thankful for what you have; you'll end up having more. If you concentrate on what you don't have, you will never, ever have enough."*

Suggested Affirmation: "I am thankful for what I have. What I have is enough for now."

Suggested Inquiry: Do I need to transform my thinking from the glass being half empty to being half full?

Suggested Action: Thank God each morning and evening for the abundance in your life.

## GROWTH

My affirmations:

_____

_____

_____

_____

What I am inquiring into:

_____

_____

_____

_____

My planned actions:

_____

_____

_____

_____

## GROWTH

*Oprah Winfrey– "So go ahead. Fall down. The world looks different from the ground. "*

Suggested Affirmation: "Just as a baby learns by falling down, I am learning each time I fall."

Suggested Inquiry: Can you see that falling can be the best thing for you?

Suggested Action: Take an area of your life in which you have fallen down and get up—exercise, eating properly, quitting a bad habit.

*Oprah Winfrey– "I was raised to believe that excellence is the best deterrent to racism or sexism. And that's how I operate my life."*

Suggested Affirmation: "I believe excellence and love are the best deterrents to racism, sexism, or discrimination of any kind."

Suggested Inquiry: Where in my life am I not pursuing excellence?

Suggested Action: Do your best today, and do better tomorrow.

## GROWTH

My affirmations:

_____

_____

_____

_____

What I am inquiring into:

_____

_____

_____

_____

My planned actions:

_____

_____

_____

_____

## GROWTH

*Oprah Winfrey– "Passion is energy. Feel the power that comes from focusing on what excites you."*

Suggested Affirmation: "I get energy through my passion."

Suggested Inquiry: How can I use my passion today to be more energized?

Suggested Action: Spend at least 20 minutes doing something you are passionate about.

*Oprah Winfrey– "The greatest discovery of all time is that a person can change his future by merely changing his attitude."*

Suggested Affirmation: "I know that I change my future when I change my attitude."

Suggested Inquiry: What attitude must I change to have my future be more the way I desire it to be?

Suggested Action: Remove a negative attitude by affirming a positive attitude.

## GROWTH

My affirmations:

_____

_____

_____

_____

What I am inquiring into:

_____

_____

_____

_____

My planned actions:

_____

_____

_____

_____

## GROWTH

*Oprah Winfrey– "My philosophy is that not only are you responsible for your life, but doing the best at this moment puts you in the best place for the next moment."*

Suggested Affirmation: "I do my best at each moment."

Suggested Inquiry: Are you responsible for your life? If not, who is?

Suggested Action: Take appropriate responsibility in an area in which you were not being responsible.

*Oprah Winfrey– "I was called to talk; to use my voice in some way."*

Suggested Affirmation: "God is calling me and I am doing His will."

Suggested Inquiry: What is God calling us for?

Suggested Action: Start by helping another of God's children.

## AFFIRMATIONS

My affirmations:

_____

_____

_____

_____

What I am inquiring into:

_____

_____

_____

_____

My planned actions:

_____

_____

_____

_____

## AFFIRMATIONS

*Oprah Winfrey– "I always knew I was destined for greatness."*

Suggested Affirmation: "God has great things for me to do."

Suggested Inquiry: What great plans does God have for me?

Suggested Action: Do God's will by helping someone. Helping someone in the name of God is being great.

*Oprah Winfrey– "I am a woman in process. I'm just trying like everybody else. I try to take every conflict, every experience, and learn from it. Life is never dull."*

Suggested Affirmation: "I am under construction, as are all of God's children, and I am enough for today."

Suggested Inquiry: Have you met anyone who is fully developed?

Suggested Action: Write down what you learned today from a mistake.

## AFFIRMATIONS

My affirmations:

_____

_____

_____

_____

What I am inquiring into:

_____

_____

_____

_____

My planned actions:

_____

_____

_____

_____

## AFFIRMATIONS

*Oprah Winfrey– "I believe that everyone is the keeper of a dream and by tuning in to one another's secret hopes, we can become better friends, better partners, better parents, and better lovers."*

Suggested Affirmation: "I follow my dreams and because of it I am a better person."

Suggested Inquiry: What are the dreams of the people you love?

Suggested Action: Encourage a loved one to follow their dreams.

*Oprah Winfrey– "I believe that every single event in life happens in an opportunity to choose love over fear."*

Suggested Affirmation: "I choose love over fear."

Suggested Inquiry: Is the choice to be fearful or loving really mine?

Suggested Action: Pray for and send love to those you fear.

*Oprah Winfrey– "I believe that one of life's greatest risks is never daring to risk."*

Suggested Affirmation: "I take reasonable risks in life."

Suggested Inquiry: What good things happened in your life because you took a risk?

Suggested Action: Take a reasonable risk today.

## AFFIRMATIONS

My affirmations:

_____

_____

_____

_____

What I am inquiring into:

_____

_____

_____

_____

My planned actions:

_____

_____

_____

_____

## AFFIRMATIONS

*Oprah Winfrey– "I believe that uncertainty is really my spirit's way of whispering, 'I'm in flux. I can't decide for you. Something is off-balance here.'"*

Suggested Affirmation: "In times of uncertainty I listen to God."

Suggested Inquiry: Who do you turn to when you are uncertain?

Suggested Action: Meditate for 15 minutes and wait for guidance with uncertainty.

*Oprah Winfrey– "I believe the choice to be excellent begins with aligning your thoughts and words with the intention to require more from yourself."*

Suggested Affirmation: "I achieve excellence by aligning my thoughts and words with intention."

Suggested Inquiry: What do you need to choose excellence?

Suggested Action: Write, think, and speak excellence in an area in which you seek excellence.

**AFFIRMATIONS**

My affirmations:

_____

_____

_____

_____

What I am inquiring into:

_____

_____

_____

_____

My planned actions:

_____

_____

_____

_____

## AFFIRMATIONS

*Oprah Winfrey– "I know for sure that what we dwell on is who we become."*

Suggested Affirmation: "I am becoming the best me there is."

Suggested Inquiry: What must you do/say/be to become the person of your dreams?

Suggested Action: Each morning visualize you as the person you want to be.

*Oprah Winfrey– "I trust that everything happens for a reason, even when we're not wise enough to see it."*

Suggested Affirmation: "I believe everything happens for a reason."

Suggested Inquiry: Review the day's happenings and discover possible reasons.

Suggested Action: Whenever possible say thank-you to God for the happenings of the day.

**AFFIRMATIONS**

My affirmations:

_____

_____

_____

_____

What I am inquiring into:

_____

_____

_____

_____

My planned actions:

_____

_____

_____

_____

## AFFIRMATIONS

*Oprah Winfrey– "What I know is that if you do work that you love, and the work fulfills you, the rest will come."*

Suggested Affirmation: "Doing what I love brings me purpose, success, and joy."

Suggested Inquiry: Inquire into the possibility that you love many things and that there is no shortage of fulfilling opportunities for you.

Suggested Action: Write down and get clear on all the things you love to do.

*Oprah Winfrey– "I don't move on logic. I move on my gut. And I have a good gut."*

Suggested Affirmation: "I trust my gut."

Suggested Inquiry: Inquire into the thought that we are endowed with unconscious competence.

Suggested Action: Get ready; fire; aim. Move, trusting that you do not have to know the logics of the situation.

## AFFIRMATIONS

My affirmations:

_____

_____

_____

_____

What I am inquiring into:

_____

_____

_____

_____

My planned actions:

_____

_____

_____

_____

## AFFIRMATIONS

*Oprah Winfrey– "I've learned not to worry about what might come next."*

Suggested Affirmation: "My trust in God keeps me from the need to worry."

Suggested Inquiry: Inquire into the statement that worrying is unnatural.

Suggested Action: Live for today. Take one day at a time.

*Oprah Winfrey– "I knew there was a way out. I knew there was another kind of life because I had read about it. I knew there were other places, and there was another way of being."*

Suggested Affirmation: "Where I am is just a starting place. I am on a journey to a better place; a wonderful place."

Suggested Inquiry: There is another way of being. How do I create another way of being for myself?

Suggested Action: Practice being different. Then be different.

## SPIRITUALITY

My affirmations:

_____

_____

_____

_____

What I am inquiring into:

_____

_____

_____

_____

My planned actions:

_____

_____

_____

_____

## SPIRITUALITY

*Oprah Winfrey– "I define joy as a sustained sense of well-being and internal peace–a connection to what matters."*

Suggested Affirmation: "I am joyful and peaceful when I am connected with my spirit."

Suggested Inquiry: Is being of service the true way to being joyful and peaceful?

Suggested Action: Visit someone in a hospital, serve at a soup kitchen, or volunteer.

*Oprah Winfrey– "In every aspect of our lives, we are always asking ourselves, 'How am I of value? What is my worth?' Yet I believe that worthiness is our birthright."*

Suggested Affirmation: "I am more valuable than I even know."

Suggested Inquiry: Ask again how you can be of value.

Suggested Action: Be of value to someone and to your loved ones.

## SPIRITUALITY

My affirmations:

_____

_____

_____

_____

What I am inquiring into:

_____

_____

_____

_____

My planned actions:

_____

_____

_____

_____

## SPIRITUALITY

*Oprah Winfrey– "It is confidence in our bodies, minds, and spirits that allows us to keep looking for new ways."*

Suggested Affirmation: "I believe our minds, body, and spirit are connected and ignoring one or favoring one is not effective."

Suggested Inquiry: How confident are you in the knowledge of your mind, body, and spirit?

Suggested Action: Do one thing today to nourish your mind, body, and spirit.

*Oprah Winfrey– "It isn't until you come to a spiritual understanding of who you are–not necessarily a religious feeling, but deep down, the spirit within–that you can begin to take control."*

Suggested Affirmation: "I am improving my spiritual understanding every day by focusing on it."

Suggested Inquiry: What do you need to do to improve your conscious contact with your spirit within?

Suggested Action: Do a 5-minute meditation.

## SPIRITUALITY

My affirmations:

_____

_____

_____

_____

What I am inquiring into:

_____

_____

_____

_____

My planned actions:

_____

_____

_____

_____

## SPIRITUALITY

*Oprah Winfrey– "Living in the moment brings you a sense of reverence for all of life's blessings."*

Suggested Affirmation: "I live in the moment and am rewarded for it."

Suggested Inquiry: Look into being in reverence for all of life's blessings.

Suggested Action: Spend time thanking God for all of life's blessings.

*Oprah Winfrey– "Real integrity is doing the right thing, knowing that nobody's going to know whether you did it or not."*

Suggested Affirmation: "I live my life with real integrity."

Suggested Inquiry: Into the statement that it takes a toll and takes energy to be out of integrity.

Suggested Action: Get back integrity by making amends.

## SPIRITUALITY

My affirmations:

_____

_____

_____

_____

What I am inquiring into:

_____

_____

_____

_____

My planned actions:

_____

_____

_____

_____

## SPIRITUALITY

*Oprah Winfrey– "What we're all striving for is authenticity; a spirit-to-spirit connection."*

Suggested Affirmation: "I always strive for a spirit-to-spirit connection with the people I meet."

Suggested Inquiry: Into the statement that letting down your mask and being who you are is the best way to have a spirit-to-spirit connection.

Suggested Action: Take down your mask and be real with the people you meet today.

*Oprah Winfrey– "Understand that the right to choose your own path is a sacred privilege. Use it. Dwell in possibility."*

Suggested Affirmation: "I honor my sacred privilege by choosing my own path."

Suggested Inquiry: What other sacred privileges do we have?

Suggested Action: Dwelling in the possibility that your path is yours to choose and that you can change paths at will.

## SPIRITUALITY

My affirmations:

_____

_____

_____

_____

What I am inquiring into:

_____

_____

_____

_____

My planned actions:

_____

_____

_____

_____

## SPIRITUALITY

*Oprah Winfrey– "What God intended for you goes far beyond anything you can imagine."*

Suggested Affirmation: "I trust in God."

Suggested Inquiry: Inquire into the possible intentions that God has for you.

Suggested Action: Stretch yourself and go a little further than before.

*Oprah Winfrey– "Be quiet. Part of your responsibility is to honor the quiet inside yourself so you can hear the call."*

Suggested Affirmation: "I honor the quiet inside me so that I can hear God's call."

Suggested Inquiry: What new ways can I become more quiet?

Suggested Action: Spend a few minutes each morning doing a silent meditation.

## PERSONAL REFLECTIONS

My affirmations:

_____

_____

_____

_____

What I am inquiring into:

_____

_____

_____

_____

My planned actions:

_____

_____

_____

_____

**PERSONAL REFLECTIONS**

*Oprah Winfrey– "I'm black. I don't feel burdened by it and I don't think it's a huge responsibility. It's part of who I am. It does not define me."*

Suggested Affirmation: "I'm _____. It's part of who I am; it does not define me."

Suggested Inquiry: How would I be if I were black/white?

Suggested Action: See through the eyes of another culture.

*Oprah Winfrey– "I've learned that you can't have everything and do everything at the same time."*

Suggested Affirmation: "I will accept what God gives me today."

Suggested Inquiry: Are you taking all that God gives you?

Suggested Action: Spend part of the day doing and part of the day having.

*Oprah Winfrey– "My first day in Chicago, September 4, 1983. I set foot in this city, and just walking down the street, it was like roots, like the motherland. I knew I belonged here."*

Suggested Affirmation: "I am in _____ and it's where I belong."

Suggested Inquiry: Where are all the places you are from?

Suggested Action: Today feed your root system by learning more about your home.

## PERSONAL REFLECTIONS

My affirmations:

_____

_____

_____

_____

What I am inquiring into:

_____

_____

_____

_____

My planned actions:

_____

_____

_____

_____

## PERSONAL REFLECTIONS

*Oprah Winfrey– "I don't think of myself as a poor deprived ghetto girl who made good. I think of myself as somebody who from an early age knew I was responsible for myself, and I had to make good."*

Suggested Affirmation: "I am responsible for myself and I am making good."

Suggested Inquiry: What does not taking responsibility give you?

Suggested Action: Do one thing that brings you a step closer to making good in any area of your life.

*Oprah Winfrey– "If you come to fame not understanding who you are, it will define who you are."*

Suggested Affirmation: "I understand who I am and that gives me freedom."

Suggested Inquiry: Into the possibility that fame can change one who is not grounded into who he is.

Suggested Action: List your values, beliefs, and interests.

## PERSONAL REFLECTIONS

My affirmations:

_____

_____

_____

_____

What I am inquiring into:

_____

_____

_____

_____

My planned actions:

_____

_____

_____

_____

## PERSONAL REFLECTIONS

*Oprah Winfrey– "When I look into the future, it's so bright it burns my eyes."*

Suggested Affirmation: "My future is bright."

Suggested Inquiry: What must you do today to make your future bright?

Suggested Action: Take one small action to make your future bright.

*Oprah Winfrey– "Though I am grateful for the blessings of wealth, it hasn't changed who I am. My feet are still on the ground. I'm just wearing better shoes."*

Suggested Affirmation: "I am grateful for all my wealth; especially the wealth that goes beyond money."

Suggested Inquiry: What is wealth? Inquire into the thought that one must stay present to be grounded.

Suggested Action: Go out with old friends. Do something to share the wealth.

## PERSONAL REFLECTIONS

My affirmations:

_____

_____

_____

_____

What I am inquiring into:

_____

_____

_____

_____

My planned actions:

_____

_____

_____

_____

**PERSONAL REFLECTIONS**

*Oprah Winfrey– "Where there is no struggle, there is no strength."*

Suggested Affirmation: "My frustrations and struggles bring me closer to success."

Suggested Inquiry: Shifting one's struggles from disempowering to empowering is in one's attitude.

Suggested Action: Spend 10 minutes working on an area in which you are struggling and are committed to succeeding at.

*Oprah Winfrey– "What I know for sure is that what you give comes back to you."*

Suggested Affirmation: "The more I give the more I get back."

Suggested Inquiry: What else can you give?

Suggested Action: Give of yourself today some money and some time.

*Oprah Winfrey– "Use what you have to run toward your best– that's how I now live my life."*

Suggested Affirmation: "I use what I have to run towards my best."

Suggested Inquiry: Into the possibility that you are limiting yourself through your conversation.

Suggested Action: Write down something you have, then use that to help you achieve your best.

## PERSONAL REFLECTIONS

My affirmations:

_____

_____

_____

_____

What I am inquiring into:

_____

_____

_____

_____

My planned actions:

_____

_____

_____

_____

## PERSONAL REFLECTIONS

*Oprah Winfrey– "Real integrity is doing the right thing, knowing that nobody's going to know whether you did it or not."*

Suggested Affirmation: "I do the right thing because it is the right thing."

Suggested Inquiry: Is God watching?

Suggested Action: Do something good without anyone finding out about it.

*Oprah Winfrey– "The key to realizing a dream is to focus not on success but significance, and then even the small steps and little victories along your path will take on greater meaning."*

Suggested Affirmation: "I see my small steps and little victories as big deals."

Suggested Inquiry: Success is a result of doing things wrong and doing things right.

Suggested Action: Do one thing that moves a dream closer to realization.

*Oprah Winfrey– "Biology is the least of what makes someone a mother."*

Suggested Affirmation: "I am a great father/mother."

Suggested Inquiry: What qualities make a mother or father?

Suggested Action: Today forgive one intentional/unintentional act.

## PERSONAL REFLECTIONS

My affirmations:

_____

_____

_____

_____

What I am inquiring into:

_____

_____

_____

_____

My planned actions:

_____

_____

_____

_____

## PERSONAL REFLECTIONS

*Oprah Winfrey– "Duct tape is like the force. It has a light side, a dark side, and it holds the universe together."*

Suggested Affirmation: "I am like duct tape. I have a light side and a dark side and together they hold me together."

Suggested Inquiry: What else is like duct tape?

Suggested Action: Today acknowledge and accept one aspect of your light side and one aspect of your dark side and then accept both.

*Oprah Winfrey– "I have a lot of things to prove to myself. One is that I can live my life fearlessly."*

Suggested Affirmation: "I live my life fearlessly."

Suggested Inquiry: What do you have to prove to yourself?

Suggested Action: Do one thing you are afraid to do.

## PERSONAL REFLECTIONS

My affirmations:

_____

_____

_____

_____

What I am inquiring into:

_____

_____

_____

_____

My planned actions:

_____

_____

_____

_____

## PERSONAL REFLECTIONS

*Oprah Winfrey– "How can I be of service? How can I use television as a service?"*

Suggested Affirmation: "Today I will be of service."

Suggested Inquiry: For whom can you be of service?

Suggested Action: Be of service to someone.

*Oprah Winfrey– "There have been times when I have been unhappy, but I realize that I created that unhappiness myself because I was so busy worrying about the next thing."*

Suggested Affirmation: "Today I am happy and am not worrying about the next thing."

Suggested Inquiry: Is worrying just negative visualization/ imagination?

Suggested Action: Take one thing you are worrying about and let it go, knowing that ninety percent of what we worry about never happens.

## LIFE AND LIVING

My affirmations:

_____

_____

_____

_____

What I am inquiring into:

_____

_____

_____

_____

My planned actions:

_____

_____

_____

_____

## LIFE AND LIVING

*Oprah Winfrey– "The more you praise and celebrate your life, the more there is in life to celebrate."*

Suggested Affirmation: "I praise God for my life and I celebrate it."

Suggested Inquiry: What are new ways in which I can praise God?

Suggested Action: Write down an aspect of your life that you are grateful for.

*Oprah Winfrey– "The whole point of being alive is to evolve into the complete person you were intended to be."*

Suggested Affirmation: "I am evolving into the person I am intended to be."

Suggested Inquiry: What is your purpose?

Suggested Action: Do something that evolves you.

*Oprah Winfrey– "Whatever you fear most has no power–it is your fear that has the power."*

Suggested Affirmation: "What I fear has no power."

Suggested Inquiry: What action can I take to overcome fear?

Suggested Action: Do one small thing that you are afraid to do.

## LIFE AND LIVING

My affirmations:

_____

_____

_____

_____

What I am inquiring into:

_____

_____

_____

_____

My planned actions:

_____

_____

_____

_____

## LIFE AND LIVING

*Oprah Winfrey– "Turn your wounds into wisdom."*

Suggested Affirmation: "I take profit from my mistakes."

Suggested Inquiry: Where in my life am I not taking profit?

Suggested Action: Take a past mistake or failed attempt and discover your profit.

*Oprah Winfrey– "Unless you choose to do great things with it, it makes no difference how much you are rewarded, or how much power you have."*

Suggested Affirmation: "I do good deeds with my power and position."

Suggested Inquiry: How can I use my position more powerfully?

Suggested Action: Do a good deed.

*Oprah Winfrey– "Every day brings a chance for you to draw in a breath, kick off your shoes, and dance."*

Suggested Affirmation: "I live each moment knowing that it is my birthright to live it up."

Suggested Inquiry: How do I live it up today in such a way that I can also do so tomorrow?

Suggested Action: Have some fun today doing something new.

## LIFE AND LIVING

My affirmations:

_____

_____

_____

_____

What I am inquiring into:

_____

_____

_____

_____

My planned actions:

_____

_____

_____

_____

## LIFE AND LIVING

*Oprah Winfrey– "Partake of some of life's sweet pleasures. And yes, get comfortable with yourself."*

Suggested Affirmation: "I partake of life's sweet moments and I am comfortable with myself."

Suggested Inquiry: Into the possibility that life's sweetest moments come when I forget myself and become fully present in the world.

Suggested Action: Set aside a specific time to smell the roses.

*Oprah Winfrey– "Getting my lifelong weight struggle under control has come from a process of treating myself as well as I treat others in every way."*

Suggested Affirmation: "With God's help, my weight and eating are under control."

Suggested Inquiry: What is God's will for me as it relates to eating and health?

Suggested Action: Establish a food plan.

**INSPIRATION**

My affirmations:

_____

_____

_____

_____

What I am inquiring into:

_____

_____

_____

_____

My planned actions:

_____

_____

_____

_____

## INSPIRATION

*Oprah Winfrey– "Take five minutes to center yourself in the morning... set your intention every day... if you don't have five minutes, you don't deserve to have the life of your dreams."*

Suggested Affirmation: "I center myself each day by setting aside five minutes for meditation/reflection/grounding."

Suggested Inquiry: Where can I make times during the day to take five minutes to ground myself as often as needed?

Suggested Action: Set aside times each day to have five minutes for reading/reflection/meditation, etc.

*Oprah Winfrey– "It took a lot of courage to take the high road, but I would rather be significant with six million people watching a show with meaning, than everyone watching a show with no meaning."*

Suggested Affirmation: "I take the high road in life."

Suggested Inquiry: How must I be to take the high road?

Suggested Action: Take a higher road in an area in which you would normally take a lower road.

## INSPIRATION

My affirmations:

_____

_____

_____

_____

What I am inquiring into:

_____

_____

_____

_____

My planned actions:

_____

_____

_____

_____

**INSPIRATION**

*Oprah Winfrey– "I came off the air and said to myself, 'This is what I should be doing. It's like breathing.'"*

Suggested Affirmation: "_____ is what I should be doing. It's like breathing."

Suggested Inquiry: What things should I be doing that are like breathing that I am not doing now?

Suggested Action: Write down activities that you are not now doing that you may want to do and notice how you feel when you write them down.

*Oprah Winfrey– "My constant focus is on being better. Should I be doing multimedia video production? Or seminars on the Internet? How can I do what I'm already doing in a more forceful way?"*

Suggested Affirmation: "I focus on being better."

Suggested Inquiry: Inquire into the question that being better starts with your speaking.

Suggested Action: Practice being better in what you do.

## INSPIRATION

My affirmations:

_____

_____

_____

_____

What I am inquiring into:

_____

_____

_____

_____

My planned actions:

_____

_____

_____

_____

## INSPIRATION

*Oprah Winfrey– "Making other people happy is what brings me happiness. I have a blessed life, and I have always shared my life's gifts with others. I will continue to use my voice and my life as a catalyst for encouraging people to help make a difference in the lives of others."*

Suggested Affirmation: "I make other people happy and that makes me happy."

Suggested Inquiry: Into the thought that the degree of happiness is a result rather than a destination.

Suggested Action: Make a difference in someone's life today.

**REGARDING MEN**

My affirmations:

_____

_____

_____

_____

What I am inquiring into:

_____

_____

_____

_____

My planned actions:

_____

_____

_____

_____

**REGARDING MEN**

*Oprah Winfrey– "If a man wants you, nothing can keep him away. If he doesn't want you, nothing can make him stay. Stop making excuses for a man and his behavior. Allow your intuition (or spirit) to save you from heartache."*

Suggested Affirmation: "I attract the ideal man/woman in my life by letting go of the men/women that are not right for me."

Suggested Inquiry: How can I change who I am being so that I no longer attract the wrong man for me, and attract the right man?

Suggested Action: Make a detailed list of your ideal man— Physically, emotionally, spiritually, values, convictions, etc.

*Oprah Winfrey— "Stop trying to change yourself for a relationship that's not meant to be."*

Suggested Affirmation: "I am the best me there is and I have no need to change who I am for any man/woman."

Suggested Inquiry: Inquire into the statement that finding the man/woman who loves me exactly the way I am is my best chance to have a successful long-term committed relationship.

Suggested Action: Get out of a relationship that doesn't work.

## REGARDING MEN

My affirmations:

_____

_____

_____

_____

What I am inquiring into:

_____

_____

_____

_____

My planned actions:

_____

_____

_____

_____

## REGARDING MEN

*Oprah Winfrey– "Slower is better. Never live your life for a man before you find what makes you truly happy."*

Suggested Affirmation: "I take my time getting to know him/her."

Suggested Inquiry: What makes you truly happy?

Suggested Action: Slow down with your man/woman.

*Oprah Winfrey– "If a relationship ends because the man was not treating you as you deserve then heck no, you can't 'be friends.' A friend wouldn't mistreat a friend. Don't settle."*

Suggested Affirmation: "I choose my friends very carefully."

Suggested Inquiry: Is being friends a critical factor in a loving relationship?

Suggested Action: Run as fast as you can from people who do not treat you as you deserve.

## REGARDING MEN

My affirmations:

_____

_____

_____

_____

What I am inquiring into:

_____

_____

_____

_____

My planned actions:

_____

_____

_____

_____

## REGARDING MEN

*Oprah Winfrey– "If you feel like he is stringing you along, then he probably is. Don't stay because you think 'it will get better.' You'll be mad at yourself a year later for staying when things are not better."*

Suggested Affirmation: "I take action and do not let the person I am in relationship with string me along."

Suggested Inquiry: Can you really change a person? Do you have the time and energy to wait for him/her to change?

Suggested Action: Check in on how you feel; if an uneasy feeling continues, move on.

*Oprah Winfrey– "The only person you can control in a relationship is you."*

Suggested Affirmation: "I work on my side of the relationship."

Suggested Inquiry: Can anyone truly control another? Do you accept the person exactly the way he/she is?

Suggested Action: Let go of wanting to control or change the person you are with, or let go of the person.

## REGARDING MEN

My affirmations:

_____

_____

_____

_____

What I am inquiring into:

_____

_____

_____

_____

My planned actions:

_____

_____

_____

_____

## REGARDING MEN

*Oprah Winfrey– "Avoid men who've got a bunch of children by a bunch of different women. He didn't marry them when he got them pregnant, why would he treat you any differently?"*

Suggested Affirmation: "Before I get involved I spend time getting to know the person to ensure he/she has the same values and commitments I have."

Suggested Inquiry: What is a more accurate reflection of who a person is–their words or their actions?

Suggested Action: Avoid problem people.

*Oprah Winfrey– "Always have your own set of friends separate from his."*

Suggested Affirmation: "I honor and keep my old friends and make new ones."

Suggested Inquiry: Having women going to women, men going to men, for support is the most effective support system.

Suggested Action: Have a dinner date with an old friend.

## REGARDING MEN

My affirmations:

_____

_____

_____

_____

What I am inquiring into:

_____

_____

_____

_____

My planned actions:

_____

_____

_____

_____

## REGARDING MEN

*Oprah Winfrey– "Maintain boundaries in how a guy treats you. If something bothers you, speak up."*

Suggested Affirmation: "One of my requirements for being in relationship is that the man/woman respects me and treats me respectfully."

Suggested Inquiry: Inquire into the thought that letting your man know how you feel is always the best policy.

Suggested Action: When the opportunity arises, use it to say what is true for you and what is right for you.

*Oprah Winfrey– "Never let a man know everything. He will use it against you later."*

Suggested Affirmation: "I say what is right for me and what is true for me after considering its effect on the relationship."

Suggested Inquiry: When is it beneficial to keep quiet about something?

Suggested Action: Before speaking ask if what I am about to say is going to help or hurt our relationship.

## REGARDING MEN

My affirmations:

_____

_____

_____

_____

What I am inquiring into:

_____

_____

_____

_____

My planned actions:

_____

_____

_____

_____

**REGARDING MEN**

*Oprah Winfrey– "You cannot change a man's behavior. Change comes from within."*

Suggested Affirmation: "I accept my man/woman as he/she is knowing that he/she is under construction."

Suggested Inquiry: Inquire into the statement that as I change, my mate changes.

Suggested Action: Focus on changing yourself.

*Oprah Winfrey– "Don't ever make him feel he is more important than you are, even if he has more education or a better job."*

Suggested Affirmation: "We are each important to the success of the relationship."

Suggested Inquiry: Is education and income important in a relationship?

Suggested Action: Tell your partner that you make a good team because you both value and respect each other.

*Oprah Winfrey– "Do not make him into a quasi-god."*

Suggested Affirmation: "My man/woman is a good man/woman and that is why we are together."

Suggested Inquiry: How do you show your man/woman how good they are without elevating him/her above you?

Suggested Action: Affirm that you make a good team.

## REGARDING MEN

My affirmations:

_____

_____

_____

_____

What I am inquiring into:

_____

_____

_____

_____

My planned actions:

_____

_____

_____

_____

## REGARDING MEN

*Oprah Winfrey– "He is a man; nothing more, nothing less."*

Suggested Affirmation: "Men are men; women are women; and viva la difference."

Suggested Inquiry: What are the significant differences between men and women?

Suggested Action: Honor the difference by treating your man/ woman like a man/woman.

*Oprah Winfrey– "Never let a man define who you are."*

Suggested Affirmation: "I am defined by God alone."

Suggested Inquiry: Inquire into the thought that when a person tries to define or box you in, they are disrespecting you.

Suggested Action: Let your partner know your personal growth plans.

*Oprah Winfrey– "Never borrow someone else's man. If he cheated with you, he'll cheat on you."*

Suggested Affirmation: "I honor and respect the sanctity of relationships."

Suggested Inquiry: When you borrow someone else's mate are you helping yourself?

Suggested Action: Turn down any offers or notions of borrowing another's mate.

## REGARDING MEN

My affirmations:

_____

_____

_____

_____

What I am inquiring into:

_____

_____

_____

_____

My planned actions:

_____

_____

_____

_____

**REGARDING MEN**

*Oprah Winfrey– "A man will only treat you the way you allow him to treat you."*

Suggested Affirmation: "A requirement for our relationship is that I be treated as an equal and be treated with respect."

Suggested Inquiry: Equal and different can and does exist in a relationship between a man and a woman.

Suggested Action: Treat all you see today the way you want to be treated, and expect the same treatment from others. Be clear that you expect to be treated with respect.

*Oprah Winfrey– "All men are NOT dogs."*

Suggested Affirmation: "I reach for the stars in everything I do, including my mate. Quality is number one."

Suggested Inquiry: Do generalizations serve you?

Suggested Action: Treat your mate as you would want to be treated.

*Oprah Winfrey– "You should not be the one doing all the bending–compromise is a two-way street."*

Suggested Affirmation: "I am accommodating and still retain my self-respect."

Suggested Inquiry: Does a commitment to meet the other person more than half way serve or hurt the relationship?

Suggested Action: Check in and compromise and bend when it is in the best interest of the relationship.

## PERSONAL AFFIRMATIONS

My affirmations:

_____

_____

_____

_____

What I am inquiring into:

_____

_____

_____

_____

My planned actions:

_____

_____

_____

_____

## TUCHY'S PERSONAL AFFIRMATIONS

Compiled by the "I Count" group - Sunday's 8:30 PM 1/30/86

1) I am lovable.

2) I count.

3) I am a good person.

4) I have a right to my feelings.

5) I profoundly and deeply accept myself.

6) I graciously accept a compliment.

7) I allow myself the proper amount of food, sleep, and enjoyment each day.

8) I easily find good in myself and others.

9) I have realistic expectations of myself.

10) My opinion of myself is more important than others' opinion of me.

11) What I need for myself is more important than what others want of/from me.

12) I don't need other people's approval.

13) I believe in myself.

14) I believe the world is a good place and I have a place in it.

## PERSONAL AFFIRMATIONS

My affirmations:

_____

_____

_____

_____

What I am inquiring into:

_____

_____

_____

_____

My planned actions:

_____

_____

_____

_____

**TUCHY'S PERSONAL AFFIRMATIONS-CONTINUED**

15) My feelings are just feelings; neither good nor bad.

16) I don't compare myself to others.

17) I am proud of me.

18) I ask for help because I am worth someone else's time.

19) I am neither wonderful nor helpless. I'm OK.

20) Looking a movie star will not change anything.

21) I acknowledge my good qualities. Not to do so would be to cheat myself.

22) I have worthwhile gifts to give others.

23) I accept challenges as a way to grow.

24) I cannot satisfy all my needs. But I am responsible to see them satisfied.

25) I deal with competition.

26) I am accommodating and still retain my self-respect.

27) I am still lovable even if I have been rejected by others.

## PERSONAL AFFIRMATIONS

My affirmations:

_____

_____

_____

_____

What I am inquiring into:

_____

_____

_____

_____

My planned actions:

_____

_____

_____

_____

## TUCHY'S PERSONAL AFFIRMATIONS–CONTINUED

28) I love others as I love myself.

29) I am where I need to be for right now. I am enough for today.

30) I say what I feel; what I have to say is important for me.

31) I am capable of defining my own limits and setting my own priorities.

32) I have a right to ask for what I want/need.

33) I will rebuild my life on the foundation of my positive traits.

34) I trust my decisions.

35) I am trustworthy: I make and keep commitments.

36) I am human; I make mistakes.

37) I have a right to be wrong.

38) To dream of what I wish I was is to waste what I am.

39) I deserve it. Why settle for less?

40) I accept others just as they are.

41) I have a right to be treated with respect.

## PERSONAL AFFIRMATIONS

My affirmations:

_____

_____

_____

_____

What I am inquiring into:

_____

_____

_____

_____

My planned actions:

_____

_____

_____

_____

## TUCHY'S PERSONAL AFFIRMATIONS—CONTINUED

42) It's OK to change my mind.

43) I take myself seriously.

44) I wear sexy underwear even when I don't have a date.

45) I'm the best me there is.

46) The only person who can reject me is me.

47) I'm responsible for my own serenity.

48) I take care of me.

49) I may not be perfect, but parts of me are excellent.

50) How I think or feel is not who I am.

51) I look at my stars, not my scars.

52) I accept my own sexuality.

53) I deserve to be.

## AFFIRMATIONS INSPIRED BY OPRAH'S WORDS

My affirmations:

_____

_____

_____

_____

What I am inquiring into:

_____

_____

_____

_____

My planned actions:

_____

_____

_____

_____

**AFFIRMATIONS INSPIRED BY OPRAH'S WORDS**

1) I reduce stress in my life by checking in with my body.

2) I trust myself. My first decisions are the best.

3) I let go by stepping back and breathing.

4) I am grateful for my body as it works for me.

5) I recharge my body whenever it is needed.

6) I cannot be defeated.

7) I am responsible for my life, and I do my best at this moment.

8) I maintain my integrity by doing the right thing regardless as to others' knowledge of my actions.

9) I can have it all in due time.

10) I hold the future in my hands.

11) I am more splendid and extraordinary than I was yesterday.

12) I am becoming the positive change I want to be.

13) I say what I want and do not put a ceiling on myself.

14) I partake of some of life's sweet pleasures.

15) I am comfortable with myself.

16) I live the life of my dreams.

17) I blossom and bloom more each day.

## AFFIRMATIONS INSPIRED BY OPRAH'S WORDS

My affirmations:

_____

_____

_____

_____

What I am inquiring into:

_____

_____

_____

_____

My planned actions:

_____

_____

_____

_____

## AFFIRMATIONS INSPIRED BY OPRAH'S WORDS-CONTINUED

18) I believe the sky is the limit.

19) I am responsible for my own life.

20) I am becoming who I need to be by letting go of who I have been.

21) I live my life to please myself, not others.

22) I do things so daring that at first I do not believe it's me doing them.

23) I believe people are who they show me they are.

24) I follow my true instincts.

25) My true passion feels like breathing to me.

26) I am always climbing.

27) I never take "no" from somebody who isn't in a position to say "yes" in the first place.

28) All things are possible because I believe.

29) I pay attention to my feelings.

30) I do not believe in coincidences.

31) I forgive and let go of wanting to change the past.

32) I love others as I love myself.

## AFFIRMATIONS INSPIRED BY OPRAH'S WORDS

My affirmations:

_____

_____

_____

_____

What I am inquiring into:

_____

_____

_____

_____

My planned actions:

_____

_____

_____

_____

## AFFIRMATIONS INSPIRED BY OPRAH'S WORDS-CONTINUED

33) I do not believe in failure.

34) I think like a Queen/King, and I am not afraid to fail. I use my failures as stepping stones.

35) I accept challenges as a way to grow.

36) I look at a new year knowing that progress will be made in all areas of my life.

37) I will do something today that I think I may not be able to do.

38) I do my best this very moment.

39) I use my energy efficiently to allow me to reach my goals.

40) The only failure is when I stop trying.

41) I know that there are no big secrets in life.

42) I realize my dreams by taking small steps and by making them significant.

43) I am the painter of my life.

44) I react to failure in a positive way knowing that my next attempt may be successful because of it.

45) I am lucky because I am prepared when opportunity knocks.

46) I put "umph" in everything I try so that more often than not I triumph.

## AFFIRMATIONS INSPIRED BY OPRAH'S WORDS

My affirmations:

_____

_____

_____

_____

What I am inquiring into:

_____

_____

_____

_____

My planned actions:

_____

_____

_____

_____

## AFFIRMATIONS INSPIRED BY OPRAH'S WORDS-CONTINUED

47) I do what I love and know that success will follow.

48) There is no such thing as failure.

49) I am discovering what I love and what my personal calling is.

50) I take the bus with others when their limo breaks down.

51) I surround myself with people better than I and who will lift me up.

52) I have friends and God to help me through tough times.

53) Inquiry: Who stands in the gap to close it for you?

54) My light comes from many different people.

55) Heaven is sharing with people.

56) My light shines within me.

57) I go the distance with my love.

58) Miss/Mr. Right is coming.

59) I touch someone's life each day.

60) I am easy to look at and easy to see.

61) I stand up for what I believe.

62) I do not give up on myself and that makes life worthwhile.

## AFFIRMATIONS INSPIRED BY OPRAH'S WORDS

My affirmations:

_____

_____

_____

_____

What I am inquiring into:

_____

_____

_____

_____

My planned actions:

_____

_____

_____

_____

## AFFIRMATIONS INSPIRED BY OPRAH'S WORDS-CONTINUED

63) My thoughts and words create my world.

64) I take responsibility for myself, and I am making good.

65) I am growing into myself.

66) I read and listen to educational programs as my pass to freedom.

67) I am always upgrading my thinking to make life more rewarding.

68) I am the best me there is and I express myself fully spiritually, emotionally, and physically.

69) I accept challenges as a way to grow.

70) I am thankful for what I have. What I have is enough for now.

71) Just as a baby learns by falling down, I am learning each time I fall.

72) I believe excellence and love are the best deterrents to racism, sexism, or discrimination of any kind.

73) I get energy through my passion.

74) I know that I change my future when I change my attitude.

75) God is calling me and I am doing His will.

76) I do my best at each moment.

## AFFIRMATIONS INSPIRED BY OPRAH'S WORDS

My affirmations:

_____

_____

_____

_____

What I am inquiring into:

_____

_____

_____

_____

My planned actions:

_____

_____

_____

_____

## AFFIRMATIONS INSPIRED BY OPRAH'S WORDS-CONTINUED

77) God has great things for me to do.

78) I am under construction, as are all of God's children, and I am enough for today.

79) I follow my dreams and because of it I am a better person.

80) I choose love over fear. I take reasonable risks in life.

81) In times of uncertainty I listen to God.

82) I achieve excellence by aligning my thoughts and words with intention.

83) I am becoming the best me there is.

84) I believe everything happens for a reason.

85) Doing what I love brings me purpose, success, and joy.

86) I trust my gut.

87) My trust in God keeps me from the need to worry.

88) Where I am is just a starting place. I am on a journey to a better place; a wonderful place.

89) I am joyful and peaceful when I am connected with my spirit.

90) I am more valuable than I even know.

## AFFIRMATIONS INSPIRED BY OPRAH'S WORDS

My affirmations:

_____

_____

_____

_____

What I am inquiring into:

_____

_____

_____

_____

My planned actions:

_____

_____

_____

_____

## AFFIRMATIONS INSPIRED BY OPRAH'S WORDS-CONTINUED

91) I believe our minds, bodies, and spirits are connected and ignoring one or favoring one is not effective.

92) I am improving my spiritual understanding every day by focusing on it.

93) I live in the moment and am rewarded for it.

94) I live my life with real integrity.

95) I always strive for a spirit-to-spirit connection with the people I meet.

96) I honor my sacred privilege by choosing my own path.

97) I trust in God.

98) I honor the quiet inside me so that I can hear God's call.

99) I'm _____. It's part of who I am; it does not define me.

100) I will accept what God gives me today.

101) I am in _____. It's where I belong.

102) I am responsible for myself and I am making good.

103) I understand who I am and that gives me freedom.

104) My future is bright.

105) I am grateful for all my wealth, especially the wealth that goes beyond money.

## AFFIRMATIONS INSPIRED BY OPRAH'S WORDS

My affirmations:

_____

_____

_____

_____

What I am inquiring into:

_____

_____

_____

_____

My planned actions:

_____

_____

_____

_____

## AFFIRMATIONS INSPIRED BY OPRAH'S WORDS- CONTINUED

106) My frustrations and struggles bring me closer to success.

107) The more I give the more I get back.

108) I use what I have to run towards my best.

109) I do the right thing because it is the right thing.

110) I see my small steps and little victories as big deals.

111) I am a great Father/Mother.

112) I am like duct tape; I have a light side and a dark side and together they hold me together.

113) I live my life fearlessly.

114) Today I am happy and am not worrying about the next thing.

115) Today I will be of service.

116) I praise God for my life and I celebrate it.

117) I am evolving into the person I am intended to be.

118) What I fear has no power.

119) I take profit from my mistakes.

120) I do good deeds with my power and position.

121) I live each moment knowing that it is my birthright to live it up.

## AFFIRMATIONS INSPIRED BY OPRAH'S WORDS

My affirmations:

_____

_____

_____

_____

What I am inquiring into:

_____

_____

_____

_____

My planned actions:

_____

_____

_____

_____

## AFFIRMATIONS INSPIRED BY OPRAH'S WORDS-CONTINUED

122) I partake in life's sweet moments and I am comfortable with myself.

123) With God's help, my weight and eating are under control.

124) I center myself each day by setting aside five minutes for meditation/reflection/grounding.

125) I take the high road in life.

126) _____ is what I should be doing–it's like breathing.

127) I focus on being better.

128) I make other people happy and that makes me happy.

129) I attract the ideal man/woman in my life by letting go of the men/women that are not right for me.

130) I am the best me there is and I have no need to change who I am for any man/woman.

131) I take my time getting to know him/her.

132) I choose my friends very carefully.

133) I take action and do not let the person I am in relationship with string me along.

134) I work on my side of the relationship.

**AFFIRMATIONS INSPIRED BY OPRAH'S WORDS**

My affirmations:

_____

_____

_____

_____

What I am inquiring into:

_____

_____

_____

_____

My planned actions:

_____

_____

_____

_____

## AFFIRMATIONS INSPIRED BY OPRAH'S WORDS-CONTINUED

135) Before I get involved I spend time getting to know the person to ensure he/she has the same values and commitments I have.

136) I honor and keep my old friends and make new ones.

137) One of my requirements for being in relationship is that the man/woman respect me and treat me respectfully.

138) I say what is right for me and what is true for me after considering its effect on the relationship.

139) I accept my man/woman as she is, knowing that he/she is under construction.

140) We are each important to the success of the relationship.

141) My man/woman is a good man/woman and that is why we are together.

142) Men are men; women are women, and viva la difference.

143) I am defined by God alone.

144) I honor and respect the sanctity of relationships.

145) Requirement for our relationship is that I be treated as an equal and be treated with respect.

146) I reach for the stars in everything I do, including my mate. Quality is number one.

147) I am accommodating and still retain my self-respect.

*–Tuchy*

**ALSO BY CARL "TUCHY" PALMIERI:**

The Platinum Rule and Other Contrarian Sayings
*(BookSurge, 2006)*

Tuchy's Law and Other Contrarian Quotes to Help You In Life's Journey
*(BookSurge, 2007)*

Off The Wall Contrarian Quotes For People In Recovery
*(BookSurge, 2007)*

The Food Contrarian: Quotes for People Recovering From or Dealing With Eating Issues
*(BookSurge, 2007)*

The Godsons
*(BookSurge, 2007)*

Josephine, In Her Words: Our Mom
*(BookSurge, 2007)*

**ALSO BY CARL "TUCHY" PALMIERI:**

Phil, In His Words: Our Dad
*(BookSurge, 2007)*

Relationship Magic
*(BookSurge, 2008)*

Money And So Much More: The True Meaning of Wealth
*(BookSurge, 2008)*

Sex and Intimacy: The Gifts of Life
*(BookSurge, 2008)*

When Man Listens: Everyone Can Listen to God
*by Cecil Rose, reprinted by Carl "Tuchy" Palmieri*
*(BookSurge, 2008)*

Relationship Recovery
*(BookSurge, 2008)*

## ABOUT THE AUTHOR

**Carl "Tuchy" Palmieri** was born in 1942 in an old mansion belonging to the former mill owner of the factory where his father worked. His family was one of six related families that occupied the mansion. The second son of Italian immigrants, Carl grew up in Westport, Connecticut. After receiving a bachelor's degree in business administration from the University of Bridgeport he began his career marketing and installing accounting computers for the Burroughs Corporation. Twenty-one years later, in 1987, he started his own computer business. Carl is also the author of a series of self-help books.

Today Carl lives with his wife, Susan, in Fairfield, Connecticut. He has three children, two stepchildren, and 12 grandchildren. His nickname, Tuchy, comes from having been one of three Carls in his family. There was a "Big Carl," a "Carl the Twin," and "Carluch," which meant "Little Carl." "Carluch" evolved into "Carlatuch," "Tuch," and finally, "Tuchy."